Go Leaving Strange

For Julie

Go Leaving Strange

POEMS

Patrick Lane

2007

HARBOUR PUBLISHING

Published by
Harbour Publishing Co. Ltd.
P.O. Box 219, Madeira Park, BC Canada V0N 2H0
www.harbourpublishing.com

Cover and page design by Mary White
Cover artwork by Drew Harris

Printed and bound in Canada

Harbour Publishing acknowledges financial support from the Government of
Canada through the Book Publishing Industry Development Program and the
Canada Council for the Arts, and from the Province of British Columbia through
the British Columbia Arts Council and the Book Publisher's Tax Credit through
the Ministry of Provincial Revenue.

THE CANADA COUNCIL   LE CONSEIL DES ARTS
FOR THE ARTS   DU CANADA
SINCE 1957   DEPUIS 1957

BRITISH
COLUMBIA
ARTS COUNCIL
Supported by the Province of British Columbia

National Library of Canada Cataloguing in Publication

Lane, Patrick, 1939–
        Go leaving strange : poems / by Patrick Lane.

ISBN 1-55017-328-6

        I. Title.
PS8523.A53G6 2004   C811'.54   C2004-901070-0

For Little Bones, the last in the sorrow-line.

CONTENTS

After

HOWL

The wolves howl with a loneliness that is only theirs.
The coyotes howl with the same wish.
The solitary loons too on the mountain lakes.
I have heard them among the hills and the far valleys.
There is no sound like theirs.
I know you cannot imagine what it is like.
I know you cannot believe anything alive can make that sound.
But you will, you will.

TEMPER

That I remember the old blacksmith tempering iron in dust and fire,
the way a blade or horseshoe struck the water, the blue flare,
a sudden quench marking the iron, an axe head's color his signature.
Along the blade of the knife he made for me, a whisper moved
as if the sun had breathed on it. He showed me the tempered whorl,
traced the waves of blue and gold with a finger thick as my wrist.
I carried the blade through the sagebrush hills and high above the lakes
stood and marked the smoke from his steady fire, the bellows deep
in the coals, setting in the sky a trade, his great hammer ringing.

I have marked the names of men on swords from the Shogunate,
on wisps of steel from Spain, the far Toledo fire still living there.
That blacksmith stood in fire for me. His hammer rang the folded iron
in layers thin as leaves and now I write the knife that it, long lost,
be not forgotten, that the sun in words be set in iron, that flames
leave as a blade a tempered breath, a blue as cold as the sun,
that a man be sure as the edge all lost knives know,
that a single breath drawn out of fire can be an iron name.

LILIES

That night smell of lilies when the moths come to make their bodies light.
Theirs are bright wings clad in pallor. They are the night and our only fear
when we sit vigil on the body in the wake room. And the white moths come
whose bodies are not made of blood. It is now we wish a fire to turn
thin wings to ash. We bring to the body our distress in quiet lament.
How like the moth's wings were my mother's hands upon my father's flesh.
In her throat was the guttural moan she called silence, her mother howl.
And everywhere are the lilies coming to life in darkness with their scent.
They are the flowers we will not have in the room where we lie awake,
our eyes white wings we fly to close, all ash upon the window
where what we see is nothing, seen again.

THE WAR

Afternoon, and the heat upon the table slipped across the melmac plates
and the steel knives and the butter, melted from the plastic saucer, slipped
to the edge of the scarred pine table and sank to the linoleum. Heat
like the pale water you see on desert roads ahead of you, the shimmer
and the mirage of a lake reflected from the bellies of clouds, you drive
through thirsty, the wheel wet under your palms. Before us water glasses
beaded from the sweat of air when the cold meets it, the home-made beer
thin with foam. He lived above Swan Lake and made pottery there,
celadon and slip glazes drawn from the yellow clay cliffs, temmoku,
the rabbit's-fur black running down, feldspar, iron, copper, and the ashes
from bones, calcium and phosphorous, ball clays and kaolin, all
for his huge hands to make into the empty containers others filled
with flowers, the vitrified glass, what he was proud of, a frail red rising
out of a deeper brown, the black, the impurities, the polluting elements,
and the beauty of his making. He was German, come over after the war,
and the same age as me, his parents dead, I think, or if not dead
then never spoken of. His hand reached through the air for bread,
broke off the crust at the end, and then he ate it, slowly, between
sips of beer. We talked the way men talked back then when they spoke
of the past, a privacy only spoken to wives and rarely then, the older days
best kept where they were in the locked leather satchel of the heart.

His was a long story that came slowly out of silence
and told without his eyes looking at me, but staring instead
out the window at the stubborn apples ripening, a pale brush of fire
flaring under the hard green. Summer in the Okanagan. The heat
and a single fly he caught in the middle of the telling, his one hand
holding what was left of the bread and his other, the left one, coming
behind the fly and then sweeping slowly, catching the fly as it rose
backwards as flies do when they first lift from what they rest on, bread,
the crumbs fallen on the slick surface of the table, a lick of wet butter.
He held his fist to my ear so I could hear the buzzing
then flung the fly to the floor, the single sharp click of its body
breaking there. And the story going on, the fly an interruption
he seemed unaware of except for the holding it to my ear
to hear its frantic wings, its sharp death, and the bread almost gone.
I spoke of the war and how it had shaped who I was, the years
forming me, had told him of my childhood and my father

16

gone to fight in Europe and of my playing what we called
as children, War. How we would choose sides, the smallest kids
the enemy, the Germans, and how we would come down on them
with our wooden rifles made from broken apple boxes
and bayonet them where they lay exposed, choosing to ignore their cries
of, It's not fair. We pushed the thin blades of our rifles
into their soft bellies, their shouts and cries meaning nothing to us
and then their tears, shameless, little kids broken in the shallow trenches
we had made in the clay hills, imagining what our fathers did each day
in the sure glory they never spoke of afterward, no matter our begging.

And his story.

That he watched his father and uncle come home to their farm
in the Black Forest, the horses pulling the short wagon in the night,
nostrils breathing mist in the cold, the wagon back piled with straw.
And the bodies of children under the straw.
That they had hunted them down in the forest, children
run from the gathering of jews and gypsies, tattered clothes and rags
wrapped round their feet. He remembered the small feet hanging
from the back of the wagon, the rags like torn flags fluttering.
His father and uncle had lifted the bodies one by one and fed them
into the grinders with dry corn and rotting turnips and blackened potatoes,
the pigs clambering over each other and screaming.
His mother had found him watching and carried him back
into the house, swore him to silence, said what she said and said again,
and he had not spoken of it these past thirty years and why
he spoke of it now he did not know, but that I had asked him of the war,
and of children playing, and that he had played too, but what games
they were he didn't remember, it was so long ago, those years, that war.
But what he remembered most were the feet sticking out
from under the straw, the horses' heavy breathing, the rags fluttering,
and his father sitting beside his uncle, tired, staring into the dark barn,
and the wagon pulling heavy through the ruts,
and the rags wrapped around the feet sticking out from the straw,
and the rags fluttering. That. He remembered that.

In the desert hills the Ponderosa pines have grown three hundred years
among bluebunch wheatgrass and cheatgrass and rough fescue, and
there are prickly-pear cactus in spring whose flowers are made one each day,

and among the grasses are rabbit-brush and sagebrush and antelope brush
where the mountain bluebird is a startled eye, the grasshopper sparrow,
and the sage thrasher, and the wood mouse and harvest mouse,
and the kangaroo rats who come out at night to feed on seeds and moths.
There are these living things, and they are rare now and not to be seen
except for the careful looking in what little is left of that desert place. And I
list them here in a kind of breathing, the vesper sparrow, the saw-whet owl,
and the western meadowlark, and the northern scorpion and the western rattlesnake,
now almost gone, the last of them slipped away into what I remember
of that time when I lived among them. I name only what I can,
my friend, the potter who lived above Swan Lake, who made pottery
from kaolin and ball clay and the glazes from the yellow clay of the hills,
and who was but a child in that far war almost no one remembers
now, the warriors dead, and the people dead, the men and women dead,
and the children dead, and the children of those warriors and those people
who remember are now fewer than they were, and that is how it is now.

Sage thrasher, wood mouse, western meadowlark, and saw-whet owl,
and the meadowlark, and the vesper sparrow, and rough fescue,
and I must tell you so you understand, that we sat there at that table
with cold glasses of beer and the remains of the bread we ate together
and he showed me how to cup my hand and come up slowly
behind a resting fly and then sweep my hand through the air
perhaps two inches from the table top, the fly who lifts backwards
when he flees, caught in my fist, and then flinging it to the floor, the click
of its body breaking there. And that I learned how to do that,
and it was important I knew what I was learning, though it was
only a kind of game between two men killing flies, and then
we went outside under the weight of the heavy sun and talked a moment,
and he did not speak of his crying at the table and I did not speak of it,
for we were men of that time and we had learned long ago not to speak
of tears and of the stories that bring them, and that in this only world
there are things that must be remembered, and that they be spoken of,
scarlet gilia, parsnip-flowered buckwheat, white-tailed jackrabbits,
and balsamroot, and the rare sagebrush mariposa, and all such things
that are almost gone, and that I can still catch a fly the way
he taught me, and that we stood there by his truck in the dust and the heat
and said nothing to each other, only stared out into the orchards
and the green apples ripening there, and then he was gone into the desert
and I can tell you only this of what I remember of that time.

WEEDS

1.

And the woolly burdock blooms in the yard and beside the gray boards of the fence
and in the wasted fields beyond and the absinthe and the nodding thistle
also bloom there with pigweed and tumbling mustard and prickly lettuce
and they are weeds and the poor live among them
and believe them flowers just as they believe the quack grass and the wild oats,
the downy brome and foxtail barley, and the witchgrass are lawns,
and the children of the poor pick the tall buttercup and the low larkspur,
water hemlock and wild carrot, death camas and yellow locoweed,
and bring them home to their mothers as bouquets
and their mothers place the blooms in milk bottles
and the children look upon the blossoms there in the kitchen and laugh
as children do when they have made their mothers happy
and then they go back out into the wasteland and play their games,
for it is summer, and it is good to be a child there on the beaten clay
among the glacial stones and broken branches of poplars and aspens
and I can see them there and part of me is made glad by their fierce joy,
and part of me is not, for I know what it was to endure there and that happiness
was rare in that world and not to be imagined or wished for. The poor
do not make wishes, for wishes are seen as luck and luck is by its nature
always bad and brings consequences and so wishes are not made,
and the small bodies of the children who do not wish and so have
neither bad luck nor good luck move in the waste places and seeing them
I am taken back to the broken bones and lice, scabs and scabies,
ringworm and roundworm and tapeworm, cuts and scrapes and bruises,
fractures, blindness, and lameness, and that the parasites and injuries
and deformities are what they know and they cannot imagine their not being there
for they have always been a part of their lives and that is how it is
for them, just as it is for their mothers and their brothers and sisters,
and the screams and the weeping in the night are also what they know
just as the beaten heads of their fathers and their huge hands and oily clothes
and the drinking and the fighting and the silences are part of them,
but there are days when the children break the thick stalks of burdock
and bring the thistle heads home in bouquets to their mothers
and those are the days when beauty is made possible and that is enough for them
for the children do not know they are poor and they do not know they suffer.

2.

And when I was a child in that world, the wasteland of barren fields,
the deserted shacks and burned-out houses, and the creeks
with the rusting bodies of Fords and Packards drowned among the cattails
and milfoil, the clasping-leaf pondweed and marsh horsetail, and mosquito larvae
in the broken bottles jutting their jagged necks from the mud,
and pieces of machinery, transmissions and oil pans, gas tanks and differentials,
bled their oil and gasoline into the puddles
where it made rainbows that would burn at the touch of a match
and my friend and I would sometimes light the edge of the creek on fire
and watch the flames reach up into the cattails
where the red-winged blackbirds had their nests
and watch the birds shriek up into the sun as their nests burned,
and in the wastelands too were silent places
where men sat around thin fires and cooked their food at night
and we were told never to go among them, though never why,
and the days were bound by the brown hills and the blue hills beyond them,
and the fires of the town dump, and the alleys of the town, which were
also our playground with their huge garbage bins and the sleeping bodies
of drunken Indians and drunken white men curled up under cardboard,
and we would roam among them, and I know we were seen as wild children,
for at seven in the morning our mothers would send us out into the world
and tell us not to return until suppertime when our fathers would come home,
and we never questioned why we were sent away and why we could not return,
for such questions were not asked by children of that time, and our days
among field bindweed and dodder and ivy-leaved morning-glory
with their white trumpets were known only to ourselves, and how we would
take the white flowers and make chains with their beauty,
and sometimes we would drape the chains around the necks of the little girls
in their cotton dresses and bare feet, and sometimes we would tear them off,
and our fires and fights, our crimes and misdemeanors, were known only
to ourselves, and such knowledge as we had of other mothers and girls,
the idiots and cripples, the deaf and dumb, the hunchbacked and the goitered,
the chinks and japs and bohunks and wops, and the rapes and tortures
we witnessed, the beatings of boys and men, and any and all of such things
that occurred in our wandering belonged to us and our interpretation of those
things, our understanding of those things, were given to us in our days
only by circumstance and event, by what happened, and never by admonishment
or praise, and never by our mothers and our fathers, for to speak was to implicate
ourselves in where we had been and what we had seen and so invite punishment,

and our silence was their silence and they told us nothing of who they were,
and so we expected nothing from them, and the only thing we knew
was that we should never bring home anything but ourselves
and sometimes not even that and never and never a mistake, never a thing
that would cost our family shame, for shame was the greatest sin and not to be
endured, and the punishment for it was not to be imagined or endured,
and that shame lived in a child just as it lived in a family,
and so we did not, for the world of our lives was without words,
and things were not spoken of, things were not said, things were left out,
and that is how it was with things, and that we knew people were things too
just as cleavers and dogbane, locoweed and puncture vine, were things,
and even the smallest child knew that, and that was how things were.

3.
And there are stories that can be told of such times and about such children
but they are long and all that is known is that things happened in those days
and there is little that can be said that will make anything clear
and there are no reasons and no excuses and no explanations
because that would mean understanding what happens inside a child
and there is no understanding what happens there,
only that there was a child,
and he was killed by his father
and he was only six years old
and I was only six years old,
and anything I might say,
anything I might write here
to explain why he was killed will not help anyone
for a child's death is a child's death
and a half century makes it no clearer than it was
when that child's father raised his huge arm in the blade of the sun.

4.
And children die and sometimes they die when you are there
and such a death brings a kind of shame that cannot be understood,
for anyone who has known shame cannot explain it and so it is just a word,
and the boy who was my friend is dead and it was a long time ago
and that is the end of it, and there is no explaining
the beatings in the shed and my watching them
anymore than I could explain why the wild carrot flower gathers itself into a clench
that is called a *bird's fist* and the fist cannot be undone without breaking it,

and that only the plant can undo itself and it only does that when it is
ready to let go its many seeds, and my friend's death is like that weed
and there is no undoing it except to say I saw him die
and that my father did nothing and my mother did nothing,
and the man who killed my friend was the father of my friend,
and I accepted my friend's death just as I accepted a dog kicked to death in an alley,
or a shot grouse in its bloody feathers or anything else that was not allowed to live,
and after my friend's death I went out alone into the secret places,
and some nights I walked among the men by the fires down by the railway tracks
and ate their food and listened to their songs,
and I don't know why I disobeyed my father,
but I know that I was afraid my father would kill me too,
and that the anger of fathers was not to be understood,
not by a child, for I remember my fear and the hugeness of my father,
his silences, the hunched shoulders and the bowed head,
and the fists his hands made, the scars and dried blood,
so I stayed far from home, far from the world where I lived,
and I went out alone into the waste places
and I learned to name the things I found there,
and that somehow I knew it was important I name things,
and why it was important I do not know now,
just that I wanted to know what things were,
and I would wander the night with weeds in my small fists
and that is why I remember burdock and bugbane,
and jimson weed and mouse-ear chickweed,
and pygmy flower and rough cinquefoil and stinging nettle and poison ivy,
and all the other names, dogberry, barberry, goat's beard, and cocklebur,
and that what happened in a family could happen in my family,
but whatever happened it belonged to the family and no one else,
and that a man's shame was his own to know,
and that what I could tell here would only be a story,
and my telling it now would have been like my telling it then,
because I had seen my friend being killed by his father and I told no one of it,
and it was because I knew that telling it would have made something happen,
the story would have led to some consequence,
and that was how it was in that world
and a little boy under the sun is a boy under the sun
and no more and no less, but sometimes there is no boy and there is only the sun.

5.

And that is how it is with stories and sometimes the teller of the story will
try to make the story better, make it more real, and sometimes leave someone
out, or describe something different from what it was, and he will say it was
a day when the sun was huge in the summer and the sky was a pale blue
because of the hugeness of the sun, and there was a creek
with cattails and duckweed and painted turtles say, and a rusted car in the water,
and the teller of the story will make the car a Ford Coupe
instead of a Nash or a Packard and no one will notice for no one is there
to correct him, for he is the only man left who knows of such things,
and everyone listens carefully, and nods their heads at the right places:
the sun in the sky, the brightness of it falling through a shed door in a blade of sun,
a stick of firewood, and a father striking his child, and the right moment to speak,
to say things, as when he places a child among death camas and yellow locoweed,
or says how a child has ringworm or roundworm or tapeworm, or has had his arm
broken by his father, or has seen a child killed by his father in a shed full of
        sunlight,
or has curled in a ball under his bed in the farthest corner of his bedroom
and held his hands over his ears to stop the shouting
and the screaming and the sound of fists
and breaking things
and slammed doors
and how the child holds his hands tighter
when everything becomes quiet in the silence that follows such things,
for that is what stories are
and that is how they happen,
and that is why there are weeds named cleavers and dogbane and puncture vine,
and that there are such things in the world, death camas and locoweed,
and that children inhabit that world, quackgrass and water hemlock,
and sometimes a child goes out into the night to the forbidden places
because he is afraid of the sun and the blade of the sun,
and there are men sitting around a stolen fire
and a child will go to them and listen to their songs
and the stories they tell of places and of the names of places
and there he will be fed beans and burned potatoes
and he will sit by the thin fires there
and return home safely with the songs and stories of those men in his mouth,
and he will try to sing them and sometimes at the corner of an old yellow house
he will stop in the night and he will stand beside blue burdocks and repeat
the sound of their song and the few words he remembers, and the story-teller

will say that sometimes now he will hear a song on the radio and it will bring back
the nights he went among those men and returned safely with their song.

6.
And that childhood remains far from us even when we are children
and to remember anything is a kind of wonder,
and to speak of it at all is to begin with names and places
and the things that inhabit them, the children and the weeds,
and so they become story, but stories are not to be trusted,
for they are like the pictures children make with crayons of a beautiful day
and there is always a sun huge in the corner of the page the child colors with
      chrome yellow
with great rays shining from it and there are green fields and round faces
though sometimes the faces do not have ears and sometimes they are without eyes,
and sometimes there is no one in the picture and the child when he is asked
says no one is there, there is no one in that world, but the sun is there,
the sun is always there, bright in the right corner or the left corner,
and there are no clouds and the sky is always blue,
and there are flowers that grow only in pictures
and the flowers are not the same as the child knows in the waste places,
but always there are children, though sometimes there are none,
and the mother of the child who makes such a picture tacks it to a wall,
or leaves it out for the father to see when he comes home, in the hope
that the father praise the beauty of what his child has done, praise the child,
and no one asks why the child in the picture of the beautiful day
has no eyes or no ears or no mouth, or why the legs and arms are sticks,
or why sometimes there is no child at all and only the sharp blade of the sun.

NAILS

Practice makes perfect, he thought his father might have said.
He stared from the window where the far voices of the monks
had reached him from vespers a few hours before, their calling
to each other the old words *mercy* and *faith* in song. He wanted
a father to have given him some small wisdom, some old song.
But his father had been dead for many years
and what memory he had was bound not by what he knew,
but by what he believed, a man say on a cross.
And then there were nails in his mind, rusted and of many sizes,
each one straightened by his own hand when he was a boy.
Far back in the century. A cold winter in a desert valley,
the poverty after the war. Who remembered it now?
His father had told him to pull all the nails
from a great pile of weathered boards
and when he had collected them in a pile
he had been told to straighten each one.
He had sat with a boulder between his knees
with a hammer too big for him, the nails coming awkward,
some rusted almost all the way through, the shafts
thin and brittle. His father had come from a time
when nothing was wasted and nothing was.
The nails were saved in green Export tobacco cans.
He still had one of the cans, had carried it with him through
death and divorce, separation and loss. He could see it hidden
at the back of the shelf behind the saws and hammers.
From the window the Fraser Valley was lost in the dark
and the pounded sickle of moon hung thin and weathered
in the southern sky. The vigil bells began and he watched the monks
move toward their night prayers, the day gone, their small cells waiting
with solitude and sleep. Men who had given themselves to God.
They were mostly old. Like me, he thought, and wondered
what would happen in the days to come, the young men no longer
bound by poverty and obedience, the monastic life at an end.
His father did not believe in words, and he smiled, remembering
how his father had signed his name, his swollen fingers
holding the delicate pen and drawing the letters, not writing them.
There were stars now and the icicle moon in the dark,
and a silence he had wanted, had come many miles to find.

I am in retreat, he thought. This is what I wanted, a monastery
far from the world. A can of nails. How strange to think of that now.
The night was cold, the vigils over now, the monks in their dark robes
slipping through the night toward their obedience. In a moment
he knew he would put on his coat and go out beyond the fields
to where the stars were but not yet. He was staring at his hands,
seeing them with a huge hammer, his fingers turning each nail
and tapping it straight, his fingers bruised, one nail after another,
the clink of metal on metal on stone, the long hours in the cold,
his father beyond him breaking with his boots the boards for the winter
upon them, the fires, and somewhere inside his hands
small child-fingers, and the nails he had carried into his life.

SHINGLE

When he was a boy he attended well to the men in the Cenotaph Park
who spoke of the war and of the friends they had known in their youth
in the rubble of Caen and Dieppe, in the camps of Burma and Japan.
Their stories were simple stories and though he knew now
much of what they told was hidden inside the words they spoke,
that their fears and shames were never voiced, still he listened,
loving most what seemed their joy.
In the cool shadows of the elm trees at noon,
on the granite steps of the Cenotaph at dusk,
the men shared their bottles of wine and beer
remembering for each other the best of days.
The boy saw them in their medals and dress, the old ones
weeping on their day, though never when they spoke
on his father's porch of the war that would surely come
that would be like all wars and the wars they had known.
The boy with bare feet and ragged cotton pants
would sit at the edge of their sprawl and listen
and sometimes know their stories were meant for him.
That meant and meaning were different by degree if not intent
did not occur to him. He could tell by their smiles they loved
the life before. What puzzled him was the moral world, though
he would not have known to call it that, and how
it never included them, that the hero of every story
was never themselves, but a man who never returned
and their hush in speaking was always to the side and not the center.
They had made themselves storytellers and took
their joy in infinite detail, as in the story of Tiny,
his father's closest friend, who burned alive in his tank
in a Holland marsh. His father spoke of the heavy water and the mud
and of a single flower floating among broken reeds, a blue flower
like a strange star floating there, small and blue as if fallen
from the sky with its broken clouds stumbling in from the sea.
It was most true because his father was not there at the dying,
his story told by what might have been, not was.

That the boy's father believed Tiny would have lived
had he been there and that what he meant was his own death
more sweetly made by sacrifice frightened the boy.
On the day his father wanted to die,
he was in southern England in a seaside town
buying brass candlesticks to send home to the boy's mother.
As his father told him the story of Tiny's death,
he took the brass down from the plate rack
polishing them absently in his hands.
He spoke of that day and the death he wished was his,
how the weather was dark upon the Dover coast
and that after he bought them they were wrapped
in cotton rags, there being no paper then.
He had placed them in his kit and walked down to the sea
and stood alone on the shingle far from the war.
Listening to his father or sitting with the men at the edge
of the Cenotaph circle, the boy learned that children
are what you leave behind, that women are never
what you have but always what you have left,
that the friendship of men was the only beauty,
that loss, not gain was the measure of a man,
and regret was in the living, not the dying.
That the teachings were in the stories
and that they were believed, that the small boy
would carry the joy of men to sorrow in this life,
and that loss was the full teaching to be learned
on the steps of the Cenotaph and in the quiet
kitchen of his home was his inheritance.
Now what remains are the candlesticks in his mind,
his father looking absently for meaning in the brass,
and *shingle*, a word he thought he knew
and meant his father when alone
stood on a wing of cedar, not on stone.

CHOICES

The apple tree in the garden is thin and black and without leaves
and the birds, the chickadees and bushtits,
siskins and juncos, come and go among its pruned
branches at dawn. It is another tree enters you in the night,
a Pinyon pine secure in the blue granite outcrop
at the top of a scree somewhere south of San Francisco
and high above the Big Sur coast, a place your body
made among stones and needles where you rested
in a hollow and stared at Rexroth's stars and saw
Aldebaran glittering in the cold night sky of his poems.

West of the west the light is pure and you look
behind, knowing what you see is everything
you have left. Constancy is what you promise. It is
what you ask the stars as they filter what light they have
through the thin air. Last night the planets lined up
and you went out to Mars and Saturn, Jupiter and Venus,
and thought you would not see them again like that
in this life. More and more you are promised less.
First light, cold iron, thin blue, the stars diminishing.

Regret is one way to understand things, your mother
bringing you Scotch Mints as you lay ill and still
faking it a bit by the narrow window that looked out
upon the Transparent apple tree with its golden fruit,
how your body still feels that thin autumn light, the red
Indian blanket wrapped around you, coughing just enough
to keep you home forever. *Golden, narrow, thin, red.*
Regret for what is remembered, *Transparent apple.*

You think for a moment you understand
that the particular can heal into what you call
proud flesh, a raised scar, white and hard,
that has no feeling, something you can know
only by touching it with the parts of your body
that still have nerves. There was the long wound on your chest
you received when you ran into a barbed-wire fence

at The United Church Summer Camp For Boys
on the beach of Otter Bay in the summer of 1948.

You picked at the scab until it grew into a long scar.
You were nine and the pain was exquisite, the blood
you licked from your fingers in dazed boyhood tasting good.
Later when you were older you told the women
you made love to you had received the scar in a knife fight
in Mexico City or Santiago or Whitehorse,
wherever you thought they would find romantic,
and how the women would touch it with their fingertips,
their gentle, tentative touch a sure sign of your suffering.

When they asked you to tell them the story of the wound
you became quiet and stared past them at the window
above the cold streets, past them into the distance
of the city you were lying in, as if what you remembered was
too terrible to speak of and how they would sometimes
kiss that scar with their lips and murmur words like:
How terrible! A feeling, you think, is what you try to achieve
and mostly fail at. A story is what you require, a plot,
where what you leave out is more important than what you tell.

It is what passes between a man and a woman,
the general, *love, pride, flesh,* and the suffering
at the heart of it, the quiet that follows the carnal, the questions
about scars, *hard, white,* so that in order to know
she is touching your wound with her fingertips
you have to see it, there being no feeling left.

In the same way, when you are reaching the end
of a poem, there is always a moment when you stop
and go back to the beginning and read
what you have written. And as your eyes travel down
through the words you begin to make the choice
that is just one of the many choices possible and you
feel a certain regret, turn to your hands and write:

The apple tree in the garden is thin and black and without leaves
and the birds, the chickadees and bushtits,
siskins and juncos, come and go among its pruned
branches. It is another tree enters you in the night
from the cold, blue, iron of the last sky. Clouds obscure
everything but the knife edge of light that rests
hard on the horizon that in a few moments will be
riddled with startled blood, what you turn away from
before it arrives, leaving to the many small birds,
chickadee, junco, siskin, the cold night sky of poems.

MY FATHER'S WATCH

My mother, drunk again, her nightgown pulled up to her hips, raised her legs and scissored them in the still air of the room where we had all lived once in the great confusion of family. I didn't know what she did there alone in the years after my father's death, what mirrors she stared into or what she saw there, what rooms she paced or where she placed her hands as she gazed into the test pattern late at night, the rye whiskey bottle beside her and the golden glass she drank from. Bare calves and thighs and the dark willow smudge of wet leaves between her legs. Daddy loved my legs, that coquette wince of voice, the sound like something dropped among steel blades and minced there. I didn't know then it was not my father she spoke of but her own. Or perhaps it was both and she was only drunk again and lost in time, her memory a face she might have known and did no longer. There are stories so simple they elude me, their meaning lost in the telling, so that even now I miss the words, the or and if, the but that makes all questions possible.

Or was it the willow above the pond
where I saw her last, that flash of red babushka
above her hands deep in the earth?

If, if, if? In time I will tell you of the wind
in the willow if you hurry to the garden,
if she is still there on her knees by the pond.

But you didn't see her, did you? So furious
her scraping at the earth, the willow flailing
in the last great winds of spring. Oh, yes.

My return to her was to a garden, the orchards of the desert hills. I would pick my steady way through the trees above the lakes in the fall until the cold branches were empty of fruit. A dead marriage, children gone, a continent to wander, and always leading back to her. What if, I might have said. Nights after the bars closed I would walk drunk the miles back to that dark house, the only light from the window a flutter of blue, the comedies and tragedies over, the news finished, the test pattern a flicker on the screen in front of the couch where I knew she sat with her whiskey and her glass. How I would wander outside saying this was the garden of my father, that is his tool shed, there is the place where he parked his car, and here is the well, the root cellar, the sawdust bin, the steps leading down into the basement—here, there, this and that, and not going, yet, into the house.

I wanted to place the word *sorrow*
in a poem so that it was no more
or less than *and, if,* or *but.*

One crow for sorrow, two for mirth . . .
I know I have it wrong, but willow leaves,
are they what fall among her slow fingers?

It is not a willow leaf, nor can it be, but that I
make of it a sorrow. The form of, how I know
the wind by the shape willow leaves make in fall.

I don't think she waited for me. I was a ghost as much as anyone was in that cold
autumn. I could tell by the way she looked at me I was a stranger kind of son. It
wasn't a question I could reach into. *Oh, it's you*, she'd say, as if there was anyone
else who might have come. I'd drink her into dawn. I'd drink her into sleep, my
body folded on the faded couch, dreams of apples tumbling from my hands into
bins that never filled. Each fall I'd come and stay the harvest month. The living
room was full of the gone, too many to count, the shadows of my family, my father,
his breathing quiet in the chair I never sat in. *That's the man's chair. Sit there, sit
there*, she'd say. I could hear his lungs hiss, quartz crystals like stars inside his chest.
When she pulled her nightgown up and raised her legs it was as if she fell backwards
into a darkness all her own and the flutter of her calves and thighs what a body does
before it dies.

So white, so white, her dance
in that room of fluttered light.

Dark earth, a staghorn's prance
among the fallen leaves at night.

How small her gentle feet, her glance,
wet willow leaves, her hands, their slight.

Should, must, will, all words. Who was it I served as I stared at her white flail and
the damp I call now leaves for lack of a better, other word, between her legs? *Daddy
loved me*, she'd say, her flirtation not with me but with some ghost that walked
inside her eyes. A father's night in that steady sorrow of straggled lipstick, the giggle
of a girl as she lowered her legs, her nightgown awry, and looked at me as if I knew.
Flirtatious, thin coquette, she stood and walked to me, and dropped into my lap my

father's watch, then swirled around the room until she slumped into my arms, a little thing, her body like a child's, thin bones and wretched flesh.

A stone fell five thousand years through ice
to find its way to this garden. First things,
where nothing is that is not nothing.

I crawl on my knees to find the trace
of her hands in the wet earth. I have a stone
to place among willow leaves and rain.

Her ghost in the garden again today.
Sleep soon, little mother. Go to spirit
that this world at last might rest.

I carried her then to the bed she had shared with my father and covered her, her face slack and wet. I sat in the light coming over the blue hills, the watch on my wrist. It had begun again, the hands starting their slow, methodical measuring. In the bracelet's chain his sweat had congealed in thin grease mixed with dust, the fragile tick of seconds counting the night into the day, my thumb moving across the scarred face and hinge of links that bound me.

TUMBLING MUSTARD

The dry ditch by the dirt road and the tattered leaves and stems
of the tumbling mustard grown spare and brittle with August
that scatter their seeds as they roll with the wind and their seeds
which remember the brown hills of North Africa and the sea
which remembers Carthage and the stones that remember
what we no longer remember, slip into the cracks of clay
and wait for the rains that will come when they come
and not before. A man has chosen not to be with a woman
and now he is standing beside the dry ditch and the wind
blows hard upon his back and he is going away to a place
he does not know. At this moment he is not trying to understand
anything and the woman who offered herself to him is not
in his mind. A tumbling mustard is caught on the prongs
of a barbed-wire fence and he is looking at the stems
as the mustard spins there in the wind, the orange seeds
falling into the cracks of dry clay. There is no one to tell
why he has refused her, except there is no rain.
He knows that the tumbling mustard came to this ditch
from North Africa and he knows that Carthage was in
North Africa and that at the end Hannibal did not live there
but in the back country of ancient Macedonia and that
he had gone there to live out his last days far from Rome,
and that the Romans hunted him down and killed him,
and that is what the man is thinking as he stares
at the tumbling mustard caught on the barbed wire
and the seeds falling. As for the woman he has refused
there is no telling, but for her brown hair and her crying,
and his going out into the heat of the day and the wind
and that somehow the mustard and Carthage, Hannibal
and the Romans, are somehow connected to the woman
and that is why he is standing there by a dry ditch
watching orange seeds fall into the cracks of dry clay.
In the wind. And without rain.

INFIDELITY

Under the rain, under the spare trunks of Indian plum,
the faded rust of redwood needles and the club moss
grown thick from the winter feast of weather. On his knees
he picks the flat needles splayed there, gathering them
in the way he remembers the monk in the old garden
gathering, his quiet in Kyoto, and leaning down after sweeping
with a bamboo rake and picking up a single needle,
placing it on a swept pile, then turning, going up
a worn path that followed the thin creek, and gone.
It was so much what he had imagined in the old poems
of Issa, a kind of stillness, perfection being
what distracts us in the moment, something forgotten
in the ordinary harmony we strive for and almost reach.
That is why he is on his knees cleaning the garden.
He is thinking of his dream, how he was gentle with her,
touching only the curve of hair above the pale shell
of her ear, the dampness there. And then the wind
and the going out into the last dark, and beginning
the clearing away, his eyes a mist, how he remembered
that, on his knees, one needle and then another, thinking
it is what the old know, a slight turning, something
not seen, and reaching back for what was left behind
on the moss, something fallen, under the rain.

BLACK DIAMONDS

Water thick with silt brought down from the mountains
and in the eddies the faint glint of what he thought once was gold,
his eyesight bad, and on his knees at the edge of the long bars
sifting through his fingers that imagining, his young sons
stumbling in their diapers, and his wife quiet on a blanket
staring out at a world gone wrong, her belly swollen, again.
Poverty is what he remembers. It was like the grass that grew
where nothing was, *poverty grass*, and so they had lived
like the grass, without substance there by the gravel bars
where the silt brought down the pyrites and rotted quartz.
It is hard to imagine now their youth. The promises left them behind
as if they had a life of their own, as if they had grown tired
and had gone on ahead in search of someone who could still
imagine. He remembers looking at her eyes, not into them,
as if he might see the animal still alive in her
and know then who she was: *poverty grass* and *fool's gold*,
the brown river huge in spring, and the trees rolling in the heave,
swept as all things were from the cliff faces far to the north away.
There is little to remember, the long days and longer nights.
It is as if when he was young there was nothing he wished
to hold onto, nothing he wished to carry into the time beyond,
the moments together when they were most alone.
He thought of their love making and how it seemed now
only punishment, short and brutal, without cries,
and then falling away into the place
that doesn't speak, the one that wants to die.
And the river, and the mountains moving to the sea
as they had moved under the ice that held them down,
and a woman on a blanket, pregnant again, staring at nothing,
and who now he wishes he knew that he might find surcease,
and to the children who stumbled in the shallows
and he remembers one day wishing they would drown,
not meaning them or anyone, just that something should die,
without anger and without love, kneeling in brown silt,
staring down with bad eyes at what the poor know is nothing,
and dreaming it anyway into another life: buying a necklace
in Woolworth's for her, Alaska Black Diamonds,

cheap glass, worthless and shining, she wore on her throat,
the verdigris turning her pale skin from white to green.

CUT-THROAT

A creek, brown water thick with spring run-off, and the trout
in the riffles come up out of the deep waters to feed. Cut-throat,
that red comma of blood, and the curl of thin water,
the elemental body, eating the eggs and larvae of insects
swept down from the banks high in the hills behind him.
When he was young he had read of a golden ring
found in the belly of a fish and standing there, so many years
later, remembering how he had thrown his wedding ring
into the same lake, he thought . . . *what?* That happiness eludes us
when we apprehend it, that the fallen world is the peculiar dialect
of the heart, that a ring flung out upon the waters will return
wearing the blood of angels in a choir of water? He
had fished there, long ago, with his young wife and
their first child. He had turned only once and saw her
pick up the baby and walk away into the willows,
her body and the body of his child
going away from him into the shade.
It is how the high waters talk to us in spring, how we cast out
with every hope imaginable, catching nothing, and casting again,
the line falling upon the waters and everything below the surface
sinking deeper, a silence waiting beyond the riffles of the creek
where it meets the lake, the good food come down from the hills.

COYOTE

He chose to eat in silence with the monks,
the oldest a man of perhaps eighty, lifting thin gruel
from a bowl, milk dribbling from his lips down his chin.
The monk's shoulders were hunched, his neck bent oddly
so his head hung over his food. Morning,
the joyful bells quiet now. He imagined the bronze
still vibrating, a sound so small only the bell could hear it,
and the stone walls and the heavy chain above it, the light
not yet striking the narrow windows of the high tower
and the cross. He had woken at dawn to the cry of a coyote,
a cadence that brought no answer but for his waking
into the night, the coyote restless, calling for a mate
who wasn't there. The monk had devoted his life to a god
who was chaste and poor and became obedient
even to the death of the cross. He wondered at the words,
not *his death on the cross*, but the cross itself a death.
The Lord be with you and with thy spirit . . . the light beyond
rose as the mountains rolled away in the slow turning
of the earth. A chickadee landed on his windowsill,
a wild life high above the bare branches of a plum.
When he was young he had thought of a place
like this, the life away from life, the one Christ
might have given had he *died to sin with him*,
had Christ plunged into the paschal mystery of his body.
The chipped statue of Saint Benedict outside his room
had a plaster duck at his feet, a symbol he didn't understand.
Perhaps like swans they plucked feathers from their breasts,
their beads of blood a memory of Christ and his sure suffering.
Or perhaps it was because they walked on water? No matter.
The old monk has given himself to god. Close to his death
he has lived as he could without sin. Such were the beliefs
he himself had turned away from, wanting something other
for the heart. Even to live in a community of men could bring
suffering, he thought, for who knew what lay beneath the old
monk's breast? Bright laughter rose from the parking lot
outside his window, young women come to the monastery
to wander the grounds, the view from the cliff
overlooking the Fraser and the far mountains white

with the last of winter snow. He wondered what they thought
to see men who lived chastely away from the world
or did they think of it at all, young as they were in their lives?
He stared down at them through the plum branches
swollen with buds, girls really, not women, not yet.
They were beautiful in their bodies, sufficient to themselves
in this time before childbirth, in this time before men
and he remembered the bellies of girls he had known
when he was young, the terrible beauty of their flesh.
How strange, he thought, the delicate bells of their voices
in this retreat he had made for the moment of himself.

THE WILD SELF

It is at the end of a life that a man may search and sometimes,
if he is lucky, know his life's meaning and so
go gratefully to his end, sure that what he has lived has mattered
in the world, the places he has lived, and the people he has known,
but there are others who sit on a beach with a piece of yellow cedar
in their hand, or a small stone, a bit of granite smoothed
by glaciers or by the rubbing of the stone against other stones,
or sometimes just by the fall and swirl of water over many years
that has worn away the sharp edges that told what it was broken from,
and the granite bears upon it a bright penumbra of white quartz
and so resembles a heavenly body and is called a moonstone,
or a piece of yellow cedar which came from an avalanche chute
high in the coastal mountains where it grew in the moist catchment
where water gathers that has come down in the dark falling of snow
and which was once made into a tea to cure insanity or used
as a *scare-away* for disease, and is the oldest of all the trees we know.

There is no understanding why a thing can stop a man in his life,
but it can, and it can be a moonstone or yellow cedar or anything else,
but most often it is a thing that comes from the sea or the land,
and so has some purity to it, some part of it retaining its wild self,
and because, even though it is broken, it is still wild,
and every man senses that, and that is how meaning begins,
for meaning comes out of such objects, the wild self comes out.
It crawls or creeps, flies or flutters, out of the thing the man holds,
and is like a snow scorpion fly, or a creeping vole, or a common bushtit,
or a great ash sphinx moth, and because, like these spirit creatures
a man sees only rarely, it is strange and mysterious, and something
the man does not imagine could be there until it appears in his eye's mind,
and the meaning draws him in to what he holds, it draws him in,
for the creatures invite him, they tell him there is something
he has hidden, something he has forgotten, and the velvet fur of the vole
whispers on his skin, and the sharp beak of the bushtit lisps
in his ear, and the fly curls into his eye, and the moth flies
into his mouth and flutters there with its great wings,
and that is when the man enters the stone or the yellow cedar
and becomes it, and it is there he finds what he searches for.

Inside the moonstone is the idea of the moonstone and it is there
that a man can sit down on a small chair beside a simple table
with only a candle stub to light his mind, just as it is inside
the yellow cedar, for there he can lie down on a narrow bed
with a red and black blanket woven of mountain goat wool
and a pillow filled with dried moss and lichens, and it is there
a man can stare up through the many rings of cedar
and see through their bands of yellow an infinite growing,
just as the man inside the moonstone can stare
through the infinitesimal crystals of granite
while around his head the halo of quartz that is the moon
shines with its bright penumbra of light, and a man
can live there inside the idea of the stone and the idea of the wood
and so know what his life has meant and know that the meaning
of his life is as the moonstone's and the yellow cedar's life, infinite
as the moment on Sombrio Beach when he stopped his life
and sat down before the waves that are always the same waves
and so always different, and look down between his legs and see
a piece of yellow cedar and a moonstone among all the many things,
the flotsam and jetsam, the bits of wrinkled seaweed and broken shells,
and pick them up, one in each hand, and stare first at one
and then at the other, and it is then that the fly and the vole,
and the bushtit and the moth appear from within the granite,
from within the many folds of yellow wood and the man
sees them and goes into the stone and goes into the wood
and knows what his life is and knows what the meaning of his life is,
that his own wild self is the wild self of the world and is infinite
and goes on forever, even into the avalanche chute of a mountain,
or onto the lip of a melting glacier that crests five thousand feet above the sea
where a stone has slept for many years and just as he arrives
the stone falls, the moonstone falls, and the man falls with it
onto Sombrio Beach where he sits staring down between his legs
at the moonstone and the yellow cedar that are his life.

THE SPOON

He has picked up the spoon from among all the small things
on the table, the knife and fork, the salt shaker you don't shake
but turn and grind, the bowl with its applesauce, the glass of milk,
and how he hesitated between the glass and the spoon, but chose
the spoon, and his daughter's voice going on
in a low and steady murmur, her blonde hair cut short
and the bit of gray at her temples,
and how he remembers his old mother hating flowers
after his father's funeral, how she would never have any
in the house, and his daughter still talking to him
in her quiet steady voice about things he already knows,
but knowing it is important for her to say them,
important for her to make some kind of order
out of what must seem to her the chaos of what will be
his life now, and the dog barking outside, and the light
on the table, and the spoon in his hands, and he turns it
over among his fingers and marvels at how his hands
have been holding spoons all his life, and he holds it
by the end of the handle and looks carefully into the shallow
bowl polished so carefully by his wife and sees there
his face upside down, and how if he could understand
the spoon everything would become clear to him, if he
could understand something this simple, something
so small and ordinary that he has used every day of his life
and never paid attention to until now, something very small,
and very simple, and not a glass, not a flower, just a spoon,
and that without it everything in his life
would have been different if there had never been spoons, this spoon,
and he feels a sense of wonder at what he holds, and he reaches out
and takes a spoonful of applesauce from the bowl in front of him
and gently, and very carefully lifts it not to his mouth,
but to his daughter's mouth, and he touches it against her lips
and she opens her mouth and it is very quiet now and the only thing
he knows he can do is in this moment, and that is what he does.

THAT COLD BLUE MORNING

Thin snow in the ruts and the men without work
rising from the ash and coals of the burner behind the mill,
the cleanup crews gone home and the long chains
no longer screaming. I wake in dreams and sweat, my mind still
shaped by a wailing woman on the sawmill road
as the trucks went by. Her song lives in me, her high thin crying,
and the girl-child in worn cotton pulling at the woman's dress,
the child's hand trembling, her mother gone mad again.
The woman's arms were raised into the river of wind
out of the north and her song rose on that wind
and was gone like the snow scoured from river ice.
The trucks went by and the men stared through starred glass,
ashamed as men were back then, the Coquihalla logs
heavy in their chains. *Good God, go home,* the trucker with me said,
his eyes straight ahead. *Jesus Christ, Jesus Christ,*
and I said nothing to what was a curse as much as sorrow.
The stories in my head are made from mountains,
they are made from cold four o'clock winter mornings,
from thin coffee in a plastic thermos, from crying brakes
and broken ruts, and from the chains and groans
of the start-up early mill, that late fifties moan of just enough
wood, just enough shelter, just enough food to live another day.
That woman on the late dawn early road was some man's
daughter, some man's wife, and though I thought
I knew the thing that drove her onto the frozen ruts,
still it had no name. *Jesus Christ, Jesus Christ,*
but it does no good but for the crying out.
I come out of the Interior and there were no words back then
but for the names of the gods and those who cried them,
staring as they did through the broken glass and diesel smoke.
Back in those nights I struggled to make words
turn into poems, but I was young and it was no good.
It was hard to make things right. My wife huddled in our bed
and there were nights I know she too might have gone
into the road to sing her only song. There were dead butterflies
and blue stones, a gut-shot doe in a spring meadow, a headless dog
in a ditch, children picking their way through garbage at the dump,
and the cold winds, and the spring breakup, and the nights

alone with words. I don't know now what drove me into poems,
what dream I had or where I was to go. I have tried to make sense
of it and so made sense of nothing. There are men who think
the stories are not them, men who've spent their lives in books
and offices. I curse their luck tonight. Tonight I place that woman
on this page in the hope she'll give me rest.
She wants her mind clear in the morning.
And me?
I want the cup and the cold coffee. I want the last of night.
I want the truck's roar and the shapes of the shadow-men
rising out of the ash and the rush of wind that follows them
when the kerosene explodes under the falling bark and wood.
If I could, I'd end her song. That's what I want.
I want the song to end that shapes me still. These words
make no sense but I write them anyway that they be said:
Jesus Christ, Jesus Christ, but the snow still blows
and the ruts freeze hard and the burner's smoke still rises gray
into that cold blue morning I used to call the sky.

WOLF

Wolf prints on the estuary and the long, slow mutter
where water breaks on sand, the broken crystals,
stone reduced to the myriad confusions we call chaos
that comes clear only when we reduce it to the few,
an eye staring into a hand that once was mountain, sand,
thin shells, and stone. And the wolf who passed through
in the night, his paws leaving a steady track, stopped
here and played a moment with a bit of driftwood
in the tidal wrack. I read the simple signs,
where he turned and leaped and turned again
like any animal in love with the dawn, his belly
full of a deer he brought down in the ferns by the creek
beyond the stand of firs and cedars. Then to play.
A solitary animal, no other tracks beyond the early
claws of crows and ravens. On a tidal stone a heron
stares down into his beard. Hunched shoulders, long beak,
he waits for salmon fry in the diminishing waters. Once,
I came here with a woman and we lay in the heat of day.
As the sun fell away she ran naked across the sand,
the sweat of her love drying on her small shoulders.
I chased her until we fell laughing on this same line of shore,
her hands and mine and the curve of her thigh at rest.
Years ago now. Here is where the wolf played
and here is where his paws turned the sand
as he turned back to the swordfern and the cedars.
I am sure it was here. That line of hills and that fir
leaning out over the waters. I am sure the tree is the same tree,
the broken crown where an eagle rested, that one branch
where the kingfisher fell into the shallows years ago.

THINGS

"The loneliness which is the truth about things."
                                    Virginia Woolf

Under the chandelier of the wisteria, hanging Christmas lights,
plastic trout and Chinese lanterns, I stare up at the dull jewels
that are the seed pods in winter, each grey carapace holding
bright flesh, and wonder at the lights I am arranging. The solstice
is three nights away and last night I stood on the deck
where dark leaves shine in their decay upon the cedar planks
and wondered at the full moon among scudding clouds,
the night's bright seed. I am late with the season's lights,
my neighbor's house glittering among the black branches
of the cherry trees and the firs. In these dark nights I hang each year
the same lights and wonder what it is I am saying.
Dickinson said, *Water is taught by thirst . . . birds, by the snow.*
Each wisteria seed shines between the folded legs of the pod,
demure, waiting for spring. Their loneliness is not ours
though we try to escape the song that draws us to them,
the mortuary of art, history telling us what we try to elude
and can't. So I hang lights that the night be made brighter,
and the seed pods hold their lips together as they wait
for the long days of spring. The rain falls and my thirst
is greater than water and no one knows where the birds sleep.
I imagine them among the green limbs of the redwood,
the branches of the firs, their small hearts beating like jewels.
That is my wish, for what the image says is always human,
and the stones we carry in our pockets are the burden
of things we have made our own. If there is snow I will know
the birds by what they leave behind. Even among words
there are bright seeds hidden; in the trees I imagine, imagined birds.

DWARF CRESTED MALE FERNS

You try to tell the truth without altering anything, a word
waiting sometimes days before appearing and even then, unsure
if it is right, if the word *whisper* is as strong as *shadow*
when it modifies a drunken junkie in a motel room:
his hand was a shadow . . . and you go to the west garden
still wondering and ashamed. You kneel among fallen needles
and plant beside a river stone the dwarf crested male ferns,
the ones you left under the cedar tree three months ago, thinking
there was time. The pale buds are the furled fists of a child's violin,
something you plant in the dream of what you think music might be
and rarely is, there being no child to play, the buds growing anyway,
pushing like clenched fingers into the mottled light, your own hands
delicate as they press the ferns into the earth at the drip-line of the cedar,
giving them a chance to live at the edge of the tree's long shadows.
The shadows whisper in the false light that blights what grows beneath.
The junkie you are writing about lived a long time ago.
The motel he is in is the kind you see now only in movies
of the fifties, the kind left behind when the highway moved,
the kind they used to name The Shamrock or Dream Away or Day's End.
The names always promised hope or escape, some kind of luck.
But the man you are writing about has gone past hope and luck
and now is working on despair, a victim in search of himself.
You ask what you feel because you know
that without feeling there can be no truth.
His hand was a whisper . . . and you think that might be closer
to what you want his gesture to be, someone small and alone
in a cheap roadside motel room with curtains that won't open,
with only a bed and a lamp and a television set that is always
tuned to the porn channel, so that when he entered the room
what he saw was a woman on her knees, her head moving up and down
like one of those plastic birds you used to be able to buy, the kind
that would bob into a glass of water for hours without stopping.
And now you know you are getting close to him, and you
return to where your poem is waiting. You think of the man
and how he lay on that bed knowing his young wife was in the hospital
three blocks away and giving birth to his child and how he passed out
and never got there, how the only thing that mattered
was his own oblivion. That cheap romance, that loneliness.

The Shamrock or Dream Away or Day's End, names
that promised peace. Something like that, a place where,
if they made a movie of the room and the man, they wouldn't use violins
and they wouldn't use ferns. They'd use a desert and a bad saxophone.
It would be years ago. You would feel him all the way down,
see him in the kind of dark a curtain makes of the sun.
His hand was a whisper, you write, a shadow in a small room.

THE MALLARD THOUGHT

> "As the wild duck is more swift and beautiful than the tame
> so is the wild—the mallard—thought . . ."
>
> Henry David Thoreau

1.
There was a time I thought monks in cloisters praying
dreamed a wild rose on the crooked road blooming
and girls in white secrets were their only wish for god.

2.
Machado said, "Making things carefully is more important
than making them." The mole in his small room
moves a small stone and waits out the rain.

3.
If the bird broken into many parts is the story of the egg
then what is the anger of the boy with no legs who spins
in the marketplace for pennies, the octave without hands?

4.
A girl glances through me. Such a cruel instrument,
such a tyranny in the strange curiosity of the invisible man
whose code of honor includes the ordinary life of angels.

5.
This bower has a wish that only a beak understands.
The "days of the good comrades" float in the puddle
where the pebbles swim among the feet of miserable boys.

6.
The "craft of life" and the placing of three leaves by the bamboo.
It is difficult to say what that meaning is, given
the moon and water, the raccoon listening for worms after rain.

DEFINITIONS

There are small blue owls in the frost, skulls I follow, each one smaller
than the last. In the garden the siskin thought is what my lover wears.
Opals, I think. But that has nothing to do with owls. Nearness. Skulls.
It is the way mice are remembered in scat. I've untangled the shape of the owl's throat.
It is always unsatisfying, everything crushed, everything what you imagine and don't.

Well, tonight there are blue owls. And frost. It is important there is frost.
And woman. It is important there is a woman. And skulls. And skulls.

But they are not important. That is what I say. There are blue owls in the frost.
This way, travel now as slow as you can. I say there will be woman and rain and
        rain and rain.
Blue owls. And happiness, happiness. And skulls, a little one the size of your eye,
so thin you can see through it to your woman walking with the sound of opals.

BREAKUP

That world is over, the river in spring when the ice went out,
a tree falling from the gravel bank into the swell of high water,
the rush of wind the branches made in their slow dying,
and the roots holding on as the body swung down river,
ice floes riding up and over and the tree breaking away,
the gouts of gravel, moss and thin grasses following the huge
drift toward the river's bend where the dead gathered
on the river bars. It is over and you will not see it again.
You will not be young again in the time of breakup.
The river song will no longer sing to you in the violence of spring.
There will be no offerings. All that is left you now is obedience.
That is what you know on your knees by the ditch.
That is your surrender.

The Addiction Poems

BITTER

Our vines have bitter grapes and we eat
and call them sweet. It is a pain in the mind,
intentional unkindness aimed only at the self.
Nitrate of silver, quinine, quassia, and strychnine,
vinegar, bad grapes grown too far north.
The caustic utterance is meant to burn. Unlike
bittersweet where you start with one
and end with the other. But you go on picking
and eating everything, horseweed and sneezeweed,
woody nightshade, monkshood, what kills you anyway
in the wrong fields of Arcady.

THE DWARF

I have mended like a dwarf with broken legs
and stand awry the sun,
beating a tin can broken with a rose.
Rise up, rise up, the world's all water now.
I spin in the changes, spin in my father's brow.
My mother is an urchin with her father's hands
scrabbling in the rags she wears to bed.
I sit in the night on a pan of beaten bronze
and turn in the circles of my love.
Rise up, rise up, I cry in the flower of light.
My brothers watch from their mesh cage in the sky.
Let him spin, let him spin, they cry.
They know.
They have a beaten turning of their own.

FIRST LESSONS

It's why women take their sons into their hands
and hurt them just a bit. Come winter, cold, and misery,
they're the ones they'll send into the hills
to kill whatever's coming wild, howling hard
in whatever gully runs to where you live.
No wonder women cry. They've got men.

DEAD BABY

Tried to lift a baby from a hole. Under the burning apples.
Raised it dead as I knew it would be. There was fire
so high the sky darkened under the flung diesel.
That was just after the war and I was just a boy.
Babies died back then and no one said a word
though you could tell by the missing eyes
what daddy kept his girl too close to him.
I dropped what I held back into that hole,
warm from the flames that rose around her.
There you go, I said, not knowing what to say.
A dead baby, me with my hanging hands,
and my brothers running in rags and patches,
going wherever there was a man could not be found.

SAME OLD, SAME OLD

My father told me of a man who climbed a tree
with a sow bear under him climbing the same speed
till there was little but a whip of limb to hang to.
Up in the dry hills back of Adams Lake.
He clung like strung grey moss as the bear chewed his calf off.
Just like that.
His runt dog who'd found the bear
and brought her back to his master barked
till he was hoarse. Feist and stupid under
that climbing-tree. The bear licked the man dead,
blood flowing steady to her tongue.
There was still country then.
I was never sure of the point my father had
when he told me that story. He told it many times
and each time he'd shake his head. Was it the dog,
the bear, or the man? What was it I was learning
knowing nothing then but cars, booze, and girls?
But then my father was in the war. It's the wonder
makes men rise to story. They tell it again and again.

SINK BLOOD

My mother said very little in her life.
I remember how, when my father
brought home something else
and slung it in the sink for cleaning,
something from water or hill, she'd say
to him, *you kill it, you clean it,*
and he'd look at her crazy.
She'd say, *I can eat them but I don't like*
hearing their song in my kitchen sink.
He never did again, just shook his head
at what she'd said. I listened once
to hear them in their bed
but didn't catch a thing, think my mother
was quiet and still much of the time.
As to my father, I don't know much,
beyond he never again brought anything
dead back into our lives except himself.

UNCLE JACK

My uncle picked me up by the back of my neck
and shoved me into my father's coffin. I was
twenty-seven years old when I kissed my father dead.
Uncle Jack worked steel and stone, his fingers
big as kubasas. My Uncle Jack, he loved my father.
I was still young enough not to know what love is.
But I won't forget my father's mouth, cold.
That's what bullets do to a family. As to my father,
he was alright. My uncle? He was mad,
but at what or whom I do not know.
He wanted me to love as much as him.
There was the powder, rouge, and lipstick,
and my face raked down my father's chest,
the hole in it singing, how everything breathed and me
trying to crawl away from those steelworker hands.

BACKWARDS

You walk backwards in time because there's more
there than anywhere. You walk into the dark
diminishing, going without grace, steadily.
You think of your bright daughter,
her hair as much silver as your own,
and you fail away, your heart spoken, broken
like grit in a grinding mill. Old
is memory gone awry, silly and foolish as cold
men are when they burn. She was so pretty
with love. You too, who in the hours
make with your seed a child
as white as sorrow, think of her. She is
tangled up in eggs and emptiness.
She shone once with you, now she is without.
Bright little dancer, singing her one song.
What you leave remains, the last light falling
like a hurt hand shaken, careful and afraid.

SWEET

There's nothing like the lick of buckshot cutting leaves
and a man swearing whose daughter cried out
in the giving night. I look at the young ones now
and think the sweet of their wild lives. But
it's when you stand and give your chest to a man
who wants to kill you. The look between your flesh.
Lead cutting leaves. Then running as hard as your hands.

AFTER

Holding a languid woman after love, her drenched
with heat and tears. *Outcry*, a word I bless.
I never wanted more, took nothing less.

ASH

She was ash-white and broken by the north,
three kids and a logger who never came home.
She was moon and wanting more, a slip of silk
she never had. When she came to me with her
artificial pearls I tore them off and they danced
like beads of sweat across the floor.
She was young and I was younger. Ash flies
in the dark. You search for fire
and mostly never find it.

SAY

I got out of the car and walked into the fog.
She was dead. I felt what I felt
and there was nothing to say to them
except say, *Stay in the car.*
And then we drove another two hours.
The fog was still heavy in the low places
so that you wanted just to fly away.
What else to say? I don't know
if that is a question, what it feels like,
a body riding up over the hood
and rolling off the windshield.
So the cop said at the end,
What a night, and I agreed,
the kids asleep in the back seat,
their mother quiet. But, you know,
just to fly off the high places
where the fog isn't there, just fly,
one of the kids, I think the oldest one,
saying, *Dad, did you kill her,*
did you kill her? And just driving,
going on home, going on home.

FATHERS

Scarlet wrist-band, a naked shoulder
where her body creeps, a curl of hair
gone small, thin salt and blind with tears.
She's picked you from the flotsam,
a glass float in search of stone. The child
she asks for comes without you, save
the open legs and lack of love.
I don't want you, she says. Later,
standing on her head in the corner
by the wrecked sofa and coke-cut magazines,
she sings a Cohen song, the one about
some lover somewhere dead. You keep
the bargain, the child but never you.
Now you wonder at her body upside-down,
where the child now man or woman lives,
the story she told of your early, remarkable death,
a car crash or knife fight or simply falling
from the back of a truck gone south.
Fathers, you say, in the seed and not the head.

SHE SAYS,

You can spend a long time
looking for the wrong man,
but you always find him.
White Feather whiskey
and money he won't spend.
She knows that
but hope will ride
forever on that promise.

CHICKENS AND VODKA

She made the best potato vodka in the valley,
bush-tempered in a clean copper coil.
Her only problem was she drank too much of it.
When I slaughtered a hundred chickens
with a short axe, swinging wild in the air,
the chickens dropping in wings and beaks,
she asked me why I did it,
standing there in her frozen vodka bones.
I told her I just couldn't bear them
burying their heads in the blood bucket.
That night she broke open the third quart
and we drank alone together brooding.
I knew there was nothing between us.
She made love like a dead animal, always
looking over her shoulder for the empty
she saw last. She took off her clothes
from the belly down, glass in her hand,
bent over and I took her as I'd always done.
It was over fast. I've seen sheep take
more time and show more love than us.
Not a whisper spilled from her steady hand,
her glass cleaving a white song in the air.
I quit next day. It was too hard
to understand, and I didn't want
to have to clean the barn of chickens,
the flies already maggots in my mind.
I still miss that vodka. Later I heard
she went with a man from the Experimental Farm
who left her with a crippled horse. God go with the horse
and go with me. I'd rather dig ditches
than walk among chickens with their heads
like mad lizards, stumbling blind with blood,
or take a woman who's mind's not on the work.

CAMPBELL'S MUSHROOM SOUP

Sometimes she's naked, wanting you.
You think about that. You look at her and all
you want to do is drift away. She cries real tears
and you know enough to stay just long enough
for her to stew cheap hamburger, gum rice,
and Campbell's mushroom soup.
Your life with her is mostly
thinking of a bar and pool table
playing for money and not for her.
That's why she cries
and that's why you keep leaving.
It's the tears and then
in the night when late you see her,
butcher knife quiet in her fist,
saying what she thinks a man won't hear:
This's the last damned man who's going to leave me.

SIGN LANGUAGE

Her left foot high in the Ontario night,
she swings her white panties like a flag.

WHISKEYJACK

A metal flume for love in the desert hills.
You love her flailing following snow water
into the apple fields, naked as a whiskeyjack.
First times cure loneliness, that waiting,
wanting. It's when she goes dancing by
herself through the dust, just alive
with her body. A man can love that,
white breasts, bronze flesh, the flume
calling out to the valley the sound of wet,
three small drops on her belly below the navel,
watching them vanish above that golden bowl.

FIGHT

I saw a man's cheek taken off by a swung hoe,
his molars shining sudden in the pickup's lights,
teeth grinding as he dropped. Wild nights, too much
liquor, wilder women, men at their steady work.

DOGS

If I owned half that dog, I'd kill my half.
Mark Twain said that. My woman hates it.
She'd give a dog her life.
Still, that black bitch mix of bull and terrier
and a bit of some gone breed is better dead.
Or let it howl alive, with only its eyes
climbing like something dead
in the nowhere hills. Here, right here,
I'd kill my half just to watch the other run.

RANGE

Town dogs will run a cow and eat her teats off
still alive in her stagger. They whine the same way
just before you shoot them, servile and ashamed,
tails tucked under, grovelling. They will pull down
anything just to see it suffer. They pack up
and run the range into the hills beyond Merritt.
You hunt them down and take their collars.
One of them I remember well, there in brass
her name, Bell, ringing her thick black neck,
blood dribble on her jowls, licking it still as she died.

PRIORITIES

Lew is going on about scars and has got to the point
where he's pulled back his sleeves to show the two
on his left wrist where he tried the blade and the one
on his right wrist where he went deep enough to die.
He's talking fast now and is just at the part where his blood
shot up so high it glued his hair to his head when a girl
walks by going wherever girls go who are that pretty
and everyone turns to watch her walking away.
He stops, his head keeping the rhythm of his words
in a steady nod so when we turn back to him
he never misses a beat, *and then* coming down
on the words like a poem he's memorized.

FACELESS

She is one of the faceless ones
and even if I try I can't
bring her to mind. The mirror
on the wall, yes, and the candle
guttering, and trying to blow
a smoke ring through a smoke ring
because I'd read it could be done
in a book somewhere.
Smoke and mirrors. Trying
and failing just for fun.
She was quiet in my hands
but if she had a name it's gone.

CURSE

Pity is hard. So is shame. I know them both
and hate myself for it. Sitting here thinking
of the beggar I pushed into a gutter. She fell hard
and cursed me in Quechua. She could have cursed me
in Spanish. It made no difference but for wondering
what a curse is in that tongue on the *alto plano*.
I knew looking at her I wasn't Jesus and never would be.
Pity or shame, they're both hard.
Which one I feel is worst.
It's what rides me now.

BUSINESS

It's the moment when you don't give a shit, surfeit
everywhere. You step through blood for a while
and then you step over it. That's when you get the big money,
looking in the gilt mirror and counting backward every cent.

WOMEN

Lines get closed and lonely and the cold
comes back like choker cable rust-cut in your hand.
I've seen my woman cruel and mostly at her kind.
You ask if we're the same and I'd say no.
I pulled burred cable through my palm
because the boss told me to.
My hand bled to bone, but still I held on
if only to save my job, my life, my home.
My woman just shakes her head at that,
wondering why I didn't just kill someone.

THE WORKING LIFE

We blew the grave with sixty-percent forcite,
the holes punched down with steel in the frozen ground.
He was old, belonged to no one and was dead.
The boss watched as they pushed him in
and back-filled with the Cat,
the curved blade tamping him down.
The boss said, ashes to ashes, dust to dust,
then stopped a second and turned away.
That's all I know, he said, *and that's enough.*

DIGGING DITCHES

Six feet down and digging not a grave.
The foreman's daughter lays her body in red dirt
and with her arm string-lean in torn cotton,
white as wax and melting, holds down a canvas water sack,
cold from riding the truck grill thirteen miles.
You look up and for just a moment don't reach.
Just look up and see her thin arm trembling.

MATCH STICK

She loves you and there's nothing
you can do. The drugs and whiskey
keep the table alive. Everyone is quiet
in the stone of their lives. You hate
her weakness, take her in the mouth,
her gagging, the rest watching,
not saying much. She curls up after,
curls up like a match stick struck.
It doesn't matter what you do sometimes.
Sometimes the night's too long.

PTARMIGAN

You break your wrist on a mountain
and things just get worse, shooting ptarmigan
with a Lee Enfield left over from the First War,
trying for head shots with one hand and nothing
working, broken birds and you frying thin blood
in a fire you hate. Seven Sisters and the far water
where you can't get to and don't want to go, salt water,
the kind you can't drink. Your truck is
three thousand feet down granite scree
and you never shot your goat. There's never
a woman there when you need her. You
fix your wrist in a splint pulled by your teeth, but
it's your bloody boots, how you can't get them off
grunting with one hand in the dark. Fire
and a woman never there again.
Dead ptarmigan, mostly breast shot.
The moon goes and rain like long black hair
falls over what you can't eat, where
you can't go, what you know won't sleep.

LEAVING OLD HAZELTON

You lie in the ditch with only the clothes on your back
and the boot where you hid the ten in the toe
is gone. You wake to the sun six miles from town.
You tell yourself when you open your eyes
you will go wherever your head points and it points
east on Highway 16. You know then you won't
see her again. You start walking the road,
boot and foot, the sock no help in the gravel.
You walk crooked and there is no help for that either.
You think of her little breasts, her thighs, but you
go on. Highway 16 moving east. Three hundred miles
before you can go south. Hitch and step, hitch and step.

JOHNNY

There's nothing clean as death and walking away.
Johnny knew that when he stole from me,
having come down off five years for manslaughter,
killing a man for a girl he hardly knew. Twenty dollars.
I caught him at the door. He was slick little then,
scratch as he was. I held his arm hard and he said,
with eyes gone dead from spite,
he'd see me tomorrow, hanging in the Blackstone Hotel.
The twenty dollars was gone as I knew it was and would be.
His body swung like meat off that hard rope hook.

KIDS AND COKE

Charley's selling kids and coke out of Barranquilla,
the boats riding north to the gringos in Miami
and you're sitting satori in the zocalo watching skirts
argue for five minutes in the alley by the church.
Money's moving like quick water. Nothing you know
got you here and you're not leaving yet.
The little one you gave bread to yesterday is gone
back to the mountains in a plastic bag.
It isn't gold and emeralds anymore.
You haven't figured it out
but you're trying hard
as you feed the soldiers dollars, Charley laughing
as he talks of Vietnam, how he loved it there,
gook skulls and heroin, telling you to write a poem
about the man in rags who gathers in his delicate hands
the words the lost ones lose when they fall into
the holes the priest makes as he chants
among incense and candles of a saving grace.
You will remember as the children go
toward the necklace of islands you'd call chains
if your brain could speak, if Charley would just
shut up, if you could remember how you got
to this new old world, a burro on its knees,
a man beating a drum, a girl whimpering,
the sun ready to drive you into the blades
of a fan and the cold mind you call a life.

IN DUE SEASON WE SHALL REAP, IF WE FAINT NOT

You lie on your belly in the scavenged bush,
the men in their bright trucks circling,
headlights hard in your eyes. Trucks
when they're hunting you take on another life.
That's what you think lying there. You say:
Jesus, Jesus, let me just this one time get away,
and mean every word. *I promise*, you say,
and then start thinking what that means
and wonder what you have that could promise
anything. Your head starts working hard.
You lie there thinking, *my woman, my life,*
and nothing adds up. But you keep on thinking,
making in your mind a deal with Christ,
your whole body into it now,
prayers flaring in your eyes. Meantimes
the trucks keep circling with their crazy lights
each curve of tire bringing them down on you
where you lie with your golden crown.

STARLINGS

He weeps by the driftwood fire,
his woman gone to sea on mushrooms,
no one knows where. Dancing naked,
the others forget everything but the coloured gods
bleeding from their eyes. He stares into the beating
water wondering. *Away,* he says, *Away*, knowing
tears are nothing to what he will find
in the morning's slack tide, everything rolling,
glass balls from Asia, beaten trees, a girl.

TRYING

I thought once the world was only forgetting.
It's like you hold a child's hand, then she's gone.
Or a wife or lover. They're there and then they're not.
So you start shaping yourself into memory
because you can't stand what it's like now, ever.
You slip inside a girl's blouse and she rises to you,
her hips lifting off the sprung seat. Your hands
can't believe what they've found. Nothing is
as soft as that, that first time. Things start,
get out of hand. Your friend takes his face
and tries to break a wall down with it.
Hammering there with blood.
You drink in a bar in some village in Ecuador
and no one touches you. No one at all.
Nor should they. You don't even have eyes.

HARE-LIP

You want someone to break your back
so you can take yourself in your mouth,
a circled snake gone rolling out of paradise
sucking your children down a hole
where no song lies. The dark ones
scream down there. I had a friend, belly-died,
who tried to find the way. When my light rose
from his crying, I stood on his tongue
and knew his death was clean as the knife
they cut him open with each Christmas
so he would talk through that hare-lip of his.
Sweet men die hard. The snakes keep rolling
in the coffins above Delphi, every lover
a man just like yourself thinking
you're safe with the wrong answer.

SMACK

Fire is how the day goes vicious, someone burning.
The baby lies in filth and you keep moving
to keep ahead of death. You'll ride anyone's life
to stay alive. Her man's gone
seventeen hours and she's still screaming as she burns
her hands slowly with the only matches left.
You watch from the beanbag, careful, thinking
there's a way out, push the baby in the drawer,
glad to see it's still alive, feet like little frogs
rising out of the smell of its only life.

SORROW

There was a girl-child small as song
sung in a room where no one but her was.
Her mother was my once or twice lover.
Her mouth tasted of blood from her lungs
and I couldn't love her enough. One day she was
gone to the bar and I woke up in the wreck
I called my body then. The girl-child came in
and sat on the floor at my feet, her honey hair
like breath coming clean in the high country.
I was barely awake and sick, naked to my waist.
She lifted up my body, barely twelve,
and touched me thinking love,
though she knew not what that meant . . . pray Christ,
I grabbed my shirt and boots and ran,
going anywhere away. I wanted her
and her just barely twelve. Love is mistaken
sometimes. Sometimes you run just out
of wanting, and not touching, her back on the floor
afraid and me so wild at what I might've done,
her crying, *What did I do wrong?*
This's for her if she ever reads it. Honey,
there is no fault a man can't fall into. It's why
it's called a fault, a crack in the rock that waits for you,
crying for love and meaning only sorrow.

BENT

There's a woman bent who thinks the world
is truth when it's all lies. She'd turn the day around
to call it night. I know her kind. There is
no suffering like hers. She doesn't know
the world is hard and cold. Bent
is what you try to straighten,
but metal breaks from weakness.
I learned when I was young to leave things wrong.
Don't work with iron when it's bent.
Men die for that false song.

CHEVYS & FORDS

Red Ford Fairlane, right fender gone, spider webs
scattered on the shield like startled hands, two fists,
one with a golden ring, the other bare, and a face
eaten by shadow, riding down Field toward the Crowsnest Pass
and East, and you clamp down, the foothills just ahead
and the flat country for a thousand miles stretching
to the Lakehead and a thousand more to Toronto
where you will cruise down Spadina to Queen and turn
west again, your 67 Ford with its Slant Six
and bald tires moving, knowing you will meet that Chevy
again somewhere near Pile O'Bones,
your fists holding hard to the road. You stop
only when you need gas and a grease of eggs,
coffee mug trembling, the waitress not looking at you
from under her bruised and beaten eyes in Medicine Hat,
then back in your car, warm vodka like oil between your legs,
Hastings & Main a place to go, if only to turn and drift
again, your eyes marking that same Chevy truck
ten miles west of Moose Jaw, no hand raised
in passing, nothing but your eyes talking to his eyes
making it the fourth time you've passed each other
in the last eight weeks of rage and knowing
he knows you through the smoke and broken glass.

HARD DAYS AND NIGHTS

There is no careful place. The world slips
and around you there are metal birds
singing the wrong songs. If I could find
a place I'd go there willingly. A dog
lies in the street with his throat cut
while around him children throw stones
at anyone who'll listen. There was a girl
I knew, but that was long ago and she is dead.
Still, I knew her. She had hard bones.
I think she loved me but I am not sure
now. Maybe it was only flesh
talking to flesh. There are women like that,
and men too, though in the lonely nights
they would all say no and mean it.
Lonely nights are not to be trusted.
We are children then and want everything.
But I remember the dog and the girl, how
she took my arm for a moment in that street
and was afraid—hard bones, hard flesh
or not, fear makes us love at times a little.

YOU WALK IN WITHOUT WORDS

There was a man I did most everything with
including kill, including women. Fresh liver
crackling on the fire and a free skirt swirling.
Ours was a different kind of sharing, her passing
one to the other. At the edge of this world
something flies up and you bring it down.
It's a startled look they get when feathers die.
Don't tell me they don't know. You walk in
from the thickets with dead birds dangling.
My friend never talked to me once for three months,
didn't talk to anyone I knew. Then that woman
lied him away. I called her Big Red. She liked it.
Him? He went out and killed seven people
one right after the other. They shot him dead
ten miles south of Nakusp on the Arrow Lakes road,
him in a stolen camper with two dead ones rolling
in the back. He played guitar like an angel,
but I blamed Big Red somehow. Something wrong
to make her let him go knowing his wont to rampage.
My friend went sideways and Big Red did nothing.
What I like to think of is the road
where it came down off the Monashee
before they dammed the lakes. There was nothing prettier,
but I don't drive it now. Not after he was gone.
I liked it when he was quiet though. All
he seemed to have was strange music.
It's what he said last to me, a willow grouse
breast in his mouth, clamping down hard.

HALF-HEARTED MOON

Sometimes I don't feel anything. It's best
to be with people when I do. I stare
across the coke and whiskey at Jimmy
and Moon. We are talking about nothing.
The half-hearted night stumbles
up the cracked pane and no one cares.
Moon is crying and there is nothing
I can do. She isn't mine
and if she was I'd leave her. Right now
I'm staring at the scar of light
cut in the sky. You may think it hard,
the part about Moon.
But she is here and she is stoned
and she's paid nothing for the trip.
She will.
The dark will come soon and eat her alive.
But not tonight.
Tonight it's just me, safe for the hours,
a bottle hidden behind the wrecked sofa,
most of an eight-ball tucked into my sock,
knowing no matter what, I'm okay.
For now.
But you tell me, if you know.

WILDFIRE

Wildfire, that ghost walking the rotted stumps.
Things dead and things not. A fire so blue.
You put your hand in the cold and walk away
in flames. Friends come and go. Women too.
I looked around just now but no one's here.
Strange how the heart never sees itself.
Wildfire ghosts and an owl step-dancing like Molly,
your hands on fire crazed blue in the gray bush.
That was before the coming down hard.
Her leaving. And you nothing if not sorry,
wildfire alive in your wretched hands.

TIGHT SMOKE

Her closed eyes talked to the walls in a bar
I don't want to remember, her man
with his one hand held to her throat
like tight smoke burning,
her broken bird wings
thrashing above the sawdust floor.
Some nights you just keep quiet. Some nights
you lean over the table and make the three
in the corner. You know she'll go
where the darkness is and there's nothing
you can do. A little thing no bigger than
a child from where you stand, held up
and shaking. Two hours from now
she'll be laughing, all the scare gone deep
inside her eyes, while you ride your cue,
lean down to a rack you know will break.

HIS OWN SWEET OWN

Trouble is hard. Not finding it is harder.
The cat close-walks the edges of the room
finding the trail out, the circuit past the strewn bottles,
a jump over the sill and gone. You go limping left,
carrying a book you don't remember writing,
find the cat licking his left paw under the plum tree,
yellow eyes like hooks in birds to come.
He's on his own sweet own.
There isn't anyone you want right now.
Not the blonde with the pull-down mouth
and not the one who cries. It's cold and early on.
The day is barely begun. In the room
there is a knife with a broken bone handle
in the freezer that's never worked, wrapped
in a pair of dirty Stanfields, put there by someone,
and on the lino floor by the mattress, a wig
you can't remember anyone wearing, long
black hair uncombed and matted. Every day
is like a number you divide that's never even,
something left over every time. Trouble
just keeps walking, crazy and clean, sideways.

THE SORROW-LINE

Sorrow comes in threes her mother says.
She shakes her head as if all she's
known is doom, three by three,
coming into her Ark of the Covenant
holding hands and singing so hard
the world might've died to hear them.
But she is the woman I love, this child,
this last one in the sorrow-line I call
Little Bones, there being in her at times
nothing but bones I pick up and hold
crying my way past the long ribs
to where her last heart burns.

CRYING TIME AGAIN

Here is the bent moon sprung wrong from Paradise
and a crazed woman whacked out by love and cocaine
keening like a knife found bleeding elsewhere
than the heart. How else to say love brought us here,
stunned and driving dumbly at the walls?
Who holds the anvil finds the hammer gone
and water when it's wrecked is mostly tears.
How hold a woman when she's gone?
I know you can beat a scythe
but it will hold no edge unless the heart is right.
Go find pure. Everything in this room is night.

HURTING SONG

Go break your heart and then with crazy glue
spend your hours healing what is broke. The blood
comes running any way it wants.
All crying is the sound.
My eyes were full of blood when you found me.
And now you expect me not to see?
Go round, go round, go round.
There was a time bad rye in winter made a woman die.
I can't stand watching a bad crop seal the hours.
What's in the fields is in your mind. Go cry.
Go heal the hurt you say you call a heart.

GO LEAVING STRANGE

You sit watching hounds go leaving strange,
their nails clicking swift the wooden floor
as they slide like narrow smoke away.
What's out there is anyone's child or beast.
They know. They have the smell on them.
You see it move in folds, the slack jowl
flutters pink and the tooth comes down
cutting stiff and the ear upraised. The door
is one way of knowing the world's gone wrong.
You let the hounds out and they go leaving strange,
even the one you call Slip tracking quick
on the heels of his wretched dam without a sound.
When a hound goes quiet into the night
you wonder. Head down and the long ears
lifting scent into the nose, she leads, he follows,
the young ones coming last, the little one
jumping vertical to see what he can't smell.
Hounds run silent till they catch the spoor.
It's why you close the door
and when your woman asks what's wrong, say
nothing, the sky inventing clouds
where no clouds are, the light in the thin pines
turning pale and the hounds lost in their steady run.

GOING BAD

You didn't take much turning to go bad.
I loved it like you'd love some girl. It stops there
mostly because we neither of us cared a damn
the world was anything but us. The black man
cocky and cool in the bar on Spadina.
I knew we had no business there. I was looking
for where I used to be and things had changed.
He called me honky so I called him nigger.
You sipped your beer, alive as anyone can be.
A woman sometimes just wants her man dead
for the hell of it. I came into you so hard back then
you'd think the world dried up and died
for want. As for the man I called a nigger,
well, we helped him home, him saying how
it was the worst thing he could imagine.
Then his woman putting him to bed.
We left with her eyes on us. There was no shame,
only anger at the man who was a boy.
Her eyes on us. She'd have killed us both.
You, you just kept turning, nuts as spring,
wild in my crazy eyes, turning hard and wild.

THE BUSH

You've drifted too far. You stare
across Babine where there are roads to take you.
Night will come soon enough. Right now
you have to decide whether to call out
to the boat and the man staring north
or crawl back into the bush and hide.

BEAUTY

Sometimes you lick a stone in a ditch to make it
beautiful, on your belly with the heat rising hard
off the swamp. It is like that sometimes, beauty.
You find it where you can. Sometimes you lie
in a ditch and lick a stone into what you know.
Sometimes the days are that hard. Sometimes
there's no other way around, heat
hard and fast and you on your belly bleeding.

WHAT YOU DO LOVE

Some nights your woman screams so quietly you wake her
gentle trying to find what animal crawls her mind. You hold on to
what's come back to you, the light from the last stars
burning cold down into the room
where she dreams herself crazed in holy flame.
Some nights are like that.
You hold her till she falls away again
and then you lie with a slit of moon so thin
your eyes can't hold it. Where you go is where
she leaves you. Some nights her dreams are what
you'd kill if you could only find the way
inside what you do love. You'd kill
to have her sleep at least happy.

PROFANE

You grow up at last and regret it all. You sit cornered
so no one can get at you, your knife in its scabbard
hanging from your belt, whetstoned to the same edge
as your eyes. There are two rifles in the truck
and miles of road. You live in a place
where a rifle is safe unlocked and loaded. There are
two Kispiox boys coming with five hundred pounds
of salmon in an hour. They don't give a rat's ass
for anyone. Don't tell me they think the world is sacred.
I've seen them dance. They dance the same as me.

BREAKING

You miss your woman when she's gone.
You sleep on her side of the bed even when
you say you won't, imagine her cut under you
like strange wool newly clipped. And fold away,
fold away. There's broken things around you
you can't fix. Blood in a boy's head and a bullet
in a man. You say grief to a chickadee
and the only tears are rain. I live too much sometimes.
You miss your woman when she isn't home.
Strange wool. That and broken things still running.

DEATH

I think of death sometimes, my own and others.
Purdy told me the worst was having no one
you could tell the story to who was there, no one
to dispute, to say that wasn't it at all, no one
to laugh in the pure knowing of it. A poet
once said *it* was the strangest word we know.
Agree or not, lonely is when the story runs out,
old is when the people do.

STILETTO

After each cigarette you save the butt stub
and store it in the old can.
When you run out of tobacco
you take out the butts, break them,
and begin rolling again,
saving each new butt. When that tobacco's gone
you go back to the can, take out the butts,
break them and roll again.
There are only twenty butts now
and you have out of them five cigarettes.
When they're gone you roll the last
five butts into two thin stilettoes.
There are five days until you get paid.
There are two butts and five days.
It's a dilemma with grief at the edges
and there's nothing you can do.
That's why it's called tragedy.
Or you could call it poor.
There's one left and four days.
You sit in the room thinking.

FORGIVENESS

You try to forgive yourself but it's not much use.
It's been lived and there's no way out
except for dying. I like the ones who choose.
I like to think of their trucks driving straight
at the concrete, hands gripping the wheel,
saying nothing to anyone. Nothing at all.

THE TRUTH

The truth is I saw what I saw,
I did what I did. So what do I feel?
I feel sometimes my heart in its cage
not screaming, just going on steady,
one beat and one beat going on.